Inventions We Use to
Go Places

Jane Bidder

GARETH**STEVENS**
PUBLISHING

A Member of the WRC Media Family of Companies

Please visit our web site at: www.garethstevens.com
For a free color catalog describing Gareth Stevens Publishing's
list of high-quality books and multimedia programs,
call 1-800-542-2595 (USA) or 1-800-387-3178 (Canada).
Gareth Stevens Publishing's fax: (414) 332-3567.

Library of Congress Cataloging-in-Publication Data

Bidder, Jane.
    Inventions we use to go places / by Jane Bidder.
        p. cm. — (Everyday inventions)
    Includes bibliographical references and index.
    ISBN-10: 0-8368-6901-X — ISBN-13: 978-0-8368-6901-9 (lib. bdg.)
    1. Motor vehicles—Juvenile literature. 2. Cycles—Juvenile literature. I. Title.
    TL147.B53   2006
    629.04'9—dc22   2006004292

This North American edition first published in 2007 by
Gareth Stevens Publishing
A Member of the WRC Media Family of Companies
330 West Olive Street, Suite 100
Milwaukee, WI 53212 USA

This U.S. edition copyright © 2007 by Gareth Stevens, Inc.
Original edition copyright © 2006 by Franklin Watts.
First published in Great Britain in 2006 by Franklin Watts,
338 Euston Road, London NW1 3BH, United Kingdom.

Watts series editor: Jennifer Schofield
Watts designer: Ross George
Watts picture researcher: Diana Morris

Gareth Stevens editors: Tea Benduhn and Barbara Kiely Miller
Gareth Stevens art direction: Tammy West
Gareth Stevens graphic designer: Dave Kowalski

Picture credits (t=top, b=bottom, l=left, r=right, c=center): AKG Images: 18b. Cody Images: 16t.
Mary Evans Picture Library: 6b, 9, 10b, 12t, 12b, 13, 14b, 16b, 19, 21, 22b, 24b. Chris Fairclough/
Watts: 10t. Ford Motor Company: 4b. National Museum of Roller Skating, Lincoln, Nebraska,
USA: 23. Topham: 4t, 7, 8t, 8b, 11, 15, 17, 18t, 20, 24t, 25. James Witham/Team Suzuki: 14t.

Printed in the United States of America

1 2 3 4 5 6 7 8 9 10 09 08 07 06

Contents

Words that appear in the glossary are
printed in **boldface** type the first
time they occur in the text.

About Inventions

An invention is a **device** or a tool designed and made for the first time. The person who designs the device is called an inventor. This book looks at some of the inventions that help people move from place to place. It also introduces inventors and shows how inventions that people use to go places have changed over time.

Making Life Easier

People invented many types of transportation because they wanted to improve their lives. It is easier, for example, to travel somewhere by car than to spend hours walking there. Cars save us time and have changed the way we live.

Linked to Each Other

One major breakthrough led people to **develop** many forms of transportation. That breakthrough was the wheel. The wheel, which was invented about six thousand years ago, made many inventions in this book possible.

Developing Ideas

The final design of an invention is not always the same as the first. Many inventions change and improve over time. The first motorcycles, for example, looked like bicycles with steam-powered engines. Steam engines were not very practical, and soon, gas-powered engines replaced them. Some motorcycles today even run on electricity!

You will find time lines throughout this book. Use these time lines to keep track of when things happened.

The time lines show, in date order, when specific breakthroughs occurred or particular inventions were introduced. Sometimes, the dates are very exact, but other times, they point to a particular historical era or decade, such as "the 1990s."

Cars

Today's cars are made of metal and, with safety belts, air bags, and padded seats, are built for safety and comfort. They run on gas, diesel oil, or a mix of fuel and electricity. Cars were not always made this way. The first cars were wooden and traveled at slow speeds.

How Does a Car Work?
A car's engine burns gas or diesel fuel and uses the energy created by the burning fuel to turn the wheels.

The Fardier
France's Nicolas-Joseph Cugnot invented the very first car, the Fardier, in 1769. The Fardier had three wheels and was powered by steam. Its top speed was 2 miles (3 kilometers) per hour.

Gas Power

Germany's Gottlieb Daimler and Wilhelm Maybach built the first gas-powered car in 1886. This car was much faster than the Fardier. It could travel up to 10 miles (16 kilometers) per hour.

Fabulous Fords

American Henry Ford was the first to build cars on an **assembly line**. This kind of mass production made Ford's 1908 Model T (*above*) affordable for people to buy. Today, the Ford Motor Company sells cars all over the world.

1769
Frenchman Nicholas-Joseph Cugnot makes the Fardier.

1886
Gottlieb Daimler and Wilhelm Maybach, in Germany, build the first gas-powered car.

1908
Henry Ford's factory in Detroit, Michigan, makes the first Model T Fords.

1930s
Adolf Hitler asks Ferdinand Porsche to produce an **inexpensive** car for the German people. By 1939, Porsche was making the first Volkswagen Beetles.

1940
Karl Probst designs the first **all-terrain** Jeep for the U.S. Army.

1997
Toyota sells the Prius in Japan. It is a **hybrid** car that runs on a mixture of gas and electricity.

Bicycles

You may know how to turn the pedals of a bicycle, but did you know that the first bicycle did not even have pedals?

Foot Power

In 1817, German Baron Karl Drais von Sauerbronn introduced the hobbyhorse. It had no pedals, **gears**, or chain. Riders sat on a wooden board between two wheels and pushed with their feet.

Bone Shakers

In 1839, Kirkpatrick MacMillan of Scotland attached pedals to the front wheel of a hobbyhorse. People could now ride with their feet off the ground. The ride was bumpy, so the machine was called a "bone shaker."

Rovers

John Kemp Starley changed the world of bicycles when he introduced the Rover Safety Bicycle to England in 1885. The Rover's pedals turned a gear wheel, which was linked to the back wheel by a chain. Like today's bicycles, the Rover's chain moved with the pedals and turned the wheels.

THE ROVER SAFETY BICYCLE (PATENTED).

Safer than any Tricycle, faster and easier than any Bicycle ever made. Fitted with handles to turn for convenience in storing or shipping. Far and away the best hill-climber in the market.

MANUFACTURED BY

STARLEY & SUTTON,

METEOR WORKS, WEST ORCHARD, COVENTRY, ENGLAND.

Price Lists of "Meteor," "Rover," "Despatch," and "Sociable" Bicycle and Tricycles, and the "Coventry Chair," Illustrated, free on application.

Trains

In countries throughout the world, trains are a fast and inexpensive way to travel. Thinking of today's trains, it is hard to imagine that the first trains were carts pulled along rails by horses.

The Rocket

In England in 1829, George Stephenson built a new steam engine train called the Rocket. It ran at an average speed of 24 miles (39 km) per hour.

Railroads in the United States

People had a hard time crossing the United States before railroad tracks were laid across the country. In the 1860s, two companies, the Central Pacific Railroad from California and the Union Pacific Railroad from Nebraska, set out to build tracks that would connect the east to the west. In 1869, workers nailed the final connecting spike at Promontory, Utah.

Terrific TGVs

The TGV is France's high-speed train. Passengers can travel at 186 miles (300 km) per hour. The TGV made its first trip in 1981, from Paris to Lyon. Other countries in Europe have built high-speed trains to connect with the TGV.

TIME LINE

1769
Scottish **engineer** James Watt develops the first working steam engine.

1803
London's Surrey Iron Railway opens the first public railroad in the world.

1804
British inventor Richard Trevithick builds the first steam locomotive.

1825
George Stephenson opens the first steam passenger railroad, the Stockton and Darlington, in England.

1890s
Electric and diesel trains begin to replace steam trains. They can travel more than twice as fast.

1964
Japan builds the Bullet train. It can travel at more than 131 miles (210 km) per hour.

Buses

All over the world, buses cover great distances. In England's capital, London, each bus travels up to 746 thousand miles (1.2 million km) in its lifetime. That is farther than a trip to the Moon and back!

See the Sights
Sightseeing companies first introduced buses to the United States in 1904. The buses could seat fifteen people and traveled at up to 20 miles (32 km) per hour.

Horse Power
France was the first country to use buses. The first buses were not like buses today. The first buses were pulled by horses.

Paris Vécu. — Une Station d'Omnibus

L J & Cⁱ⁰. éd

Steam Engines

In 1829, Sir Goldsworthy Gurney of England made a steam-powered coach (*below*). Although his steam coach traveled faster than a horse-drawn bus, not many of them were made because drivers had to pay a fee to use them on the roads in England.

Just Like Cars

In the early 1900s, when car engines were being developed, gas-powered buses replaced steam buses. During the same period, people started adding covered roofs and rubber tires to make buses more comfortable.

TIME LINE

1820s
Horses pull buses in France.

1829
George Shillibeer runs the first British bus service in London.

Abraham Brower starts the first U.S. bus route in New York City.

1904
Scotland Yard licenses the first gas-powered bus in London.

The first sightseeing buses travel in the United States.

1914
Greyhound buses begin taking passengers from city to city in Minnesota.

1920s
People make buses with covered roofs and rubber tires.

Motorcycles

Some motorcycles can travel faster than 160 miles (257 km) per hour, so it may be hard to imagine that some of the early motorcycles could only travel 7 miles (11 km) per hour.

Sylvester Howard Roper's Motorcycle

In 1867, Sylvester Howard Roper demonstrated his steam-powered motorcycle in Roxbury, Massachusetts. It was not very practical because its engine used a lot of **coal**.

The Father of the Motorcycle

In 1885, German engineer Gottlieb Daimler attached a small gas engine to a wooden bicycle frame. His invention became popular and earned him the nickname "the father of the motorcycle."

steering lever

motor

seat

steady wheels

Harley-Davidson

William Harley and Arthur Davidson built and sold their first racing motorcycle in Milwaukee, Wisconsin, in 1903. By 1914, Harley-Davidson motorcycles started to win so many racing **competitions** that they became known as the "Wrecking Crew."

TIME LINE

1867
Sylvester Howard Roper designs the first steam motorcycle in Massachusetts.

1885
Gottlieb Daimler attaches a gas engine to a bicycle frame.

1894
The Hildebrand and Wolfmueller company of Germany produces the first motorcycles for public purchase.

1903
William Harley and Arthur Davidson start the Harley-Davidson Motor Company in a shed in Wisconsin and build their first racing motorcycle.

2005
Located in Pennsylvania, the company eCycle begins testing a hybrid motorcycle that runs on electricity.

Airplanes

Inventors had been trying to make flying machines from as early as 400 B.C. Greek legends claim the Greek scholar Archytas built a wooden pigeon that moved through the air with steam. Since then, flying machines have come a long way.

Over the Sea
In 1927, U.S. **aviator** Charles Lindbergh piloted the first nonstop **solo** flight across the Atlantic Ocean. He flew from New York to Paris in 33.5 hours.

Flying Around

In 1903, Orville and Wilbur Wright designed the first successful airplane. Their first flight in North Carolina lasted twelve seconds.

Brilliant Boeings

In 1969, Boeing built the first 747 jet (*far left*) in Washington State. At the time, the 747 was the largest passenger airplane in the world. People called it the "Jumbo Jet." The first 747 could carry more than four hundred people and could fly 640 miles (1,030 km) per hour. Many airplanes today are modeled after the 747 jet.

Concorde

In 1976, France's Concorde was the world's first airplane to fly passengers faster than the speed of sound. The **supersonic** Concordes were used until 2003, when they were taken out of service.

TIME LINE

1903
The Wright brothers fly the first airplane.

1909
France's Louis Blériot is the first to fly across the English Channel.

1927
Charles Lindbergh flies across the Atlantic Ocean.

1928
U.S. aviator Amelia Earhart is the first woman to fly across the Atlantic.

1939
German Hans von Ohain's Heinkel He178 is the first jet engine to fly.

1960
Hawker P.1127, in England, makes the first vertical takeoffs and landings.

2005
The Airbus A380 becomes the largest airplane in the world. It can carry more than 550 passengers.

Wheelchairs

The ancient Greeks may have used a type of wheelchair as long ago as 530 B.C. Wheelchairs have changed a lot since then, including the three-wheeled models that athletes use in competitions.

Farfler's Wheel Chair

In 1655 in Germany, Stephen Farfler, a **paraplegic**, designed his own wheelchair. His wheelchair allowed him to travel from place to place by using his arms, so that he did not need someone to push him.

Paralympics
The first Olympic-style games for disabled athletes were held in Rome in 1960. Today, the Paralympic Games include basketball, tennis, rugby, and more for wheelchair athletes.

18

Bath Chairs

In 1783, John Dawson developed the first wheelchair that was sold to the public. People called it the Bath chair (*below*) after Dawson's home town in England.

Folding Chairs

In California in 1933, mechanical engineer Harry Jennings developed a folding wheelchair with his friend Herbert Everest, an injured mining engineer. Their design was easy to carry around because it could be folded and put into a car. This chair became the model for modern folding wheelchairs.

TIME LINE

530 B.C.
A picture on a Greek vase shows the first furniture with wheels.

1595
Spain's King Philip II uses a special "**invalid**'s chair."

1918
George Westinghouse **patents** an electric wheelchair in New York.

1933
Franklin D. Roosevelt is the first U.S. president to use a wheelchair.

1948
The Stoke Mandeville Games in England become the first sporting event for wheelchair users.

1979
The first lightweight wheelchair, called the "Quickie," is introduced.

2003
The iBOT® wheelchair can climb stairs!

Motor Scooters

Sometimes, one invention leads to another. People developed motor scooters, for example, after motorcycles. Motor scooters became popular because people could travel without using much gas.

The Autoped

Some **historians** credit the Autoped Company of America, in New York, for developing the first motor scooter. Introduced in 1918, it had no seat, so the rider had to stand while operating the **steering column**. Early scooters could travel 10 miles (16 km) per hour.

Parascooting
During World War II, armies used parachutes to drop scooters near their troops to help the troops move more quickly from one place to another.

The Wasp

Soon after World War II, the Piaggio airplane factory in Italy developed the Vespa scooter. When the company's owner, Enrico Piaggio first saw the scooter, he exclaimed, "Sembra una vespa!" ("It looks like a wasp!")

Lambretta Scooters

Ferdinando Innocenti's Italian company made the Lambretta (*above*) in 1947. The Lambretta had a second seat, making it an inexpensive way to carry passengers.

Roller Skates

Most people use roller skates for fun, but the first roller skates were used for transportation in Holland — as "ice skates" for summer.

Roll Away

No one knows the name of Holland's first roller skate inventor, but the first recorded inventor of roller skates was Jean-Joseph Merlin of Belgium. In 1760, Merlin wore his metal-wheeled, **in-line** skate boots to show to guests at a party. He had not yet found a way to stop, however, and he crashed into a mirror.

Get Your Skates On!

In 1863, James L. Plimpton designed a **quad** roller skate.  It had two pairs of wheels, on the heel and the toe, making it easier for skaters to turn. In 1866, he opened his own skating rink in New York City.

In 1884, Levant Richardson, of Chicago, Illinois, made roller skates go faster and more smoothly by adding steel ball bearings to the wheels.

Ball Bearings
Ball bearings are tiny steel balls that fit between a wheel and an **axle**. They help the wheel move smoothly.

Back In-Line

In 1980, two brothers from Minnesota, Scott and Brennan Olson, found an old pair of in-line skates and improved the design to use them for summer hockey practice. They founded Rollerblade, Inc., to produce their in-line skates.

TIME LINE

1700s
An unknown Dutchman attaches wooden spools to boards under his shoes to make rolling wheels for skates.

1760
Jean-Joseph Merlin crashes into a mirror while wearing the roller skates he invented.

1863
James Plimpton designs the quad skate.

1884
Levant Richardson patents ball bearings.

1960s
Plastic wheels make roller skates lighter and easier to use.

1980
Scott and Brennan Olson bring back in-line roller skates with Rollerblades.

Helicopters

Helicopters are amazing flying machines. Their blades turn very fast to make them move, and because they can take off and land vertically, or straight up and down, they can fly through small spaces.

First Flight

In 1907, Paul Cornu of France built the first helicopter to leave the ground. His machine flew only for a few seconds. As with many inventions, many other people worked on the design before helicopters could fly for long distances.

Sikorsky's Success

Russia's Igor Sikorsky designed one of the most successful helicopters. He started working on helicopters in 1909. By 1940, Sikorsky had made the VS-300, which worked the best. Because the VS-300 served as a model for many helicopters after it, Sikorsky is known as the "father of helicopters."

Westland Lynx

In 1971, Britain's Westland Lynx helicopter flew for the first time. In 1986, a Westland Lynx broke the world record for helicopter speed by flying 250 miles (401 km) per hour. Today, more than a dozen countries, including Brazil, France, and Nigeria, use Westland Lynx for their military helicopters.

TIME LINE

300s
A Chinese flying toy has a **rotary** wing design.

1490s
Leonardo Da Vinci sketches an idea for a helicopter.

1907
France's Paul Cornu builds the first working helicopter.

1924
France's Etienne Oehmichen flies a helicopter for 0.6 miles (1 km).

1986
Westland Lynx breaks the world helicopter speed record.

More Inventions

Every day, people use many forms of transportation. Adults use strollers, for example, to push children from place to place, and many people use boats or ferries to travel to work or to go on vacation.

Baby Strollers

It is difficult for parents to go places with children, especially if the children are too small to walk. In 1733, England's William Kent designed the first baby buggy. Englishman Owen Maclaren made baby buggies even better in 1965, when he created a stroller that could be folded up.

Ferries

Boats have been used to carry people short distances across water for thousands of years. Today, ferries transport people, bicycles, cars, and even trucks. The first steam-powered ferry crossed between Manhattan and Brooklyn, New York, in 1814.

Push Scooters

Children have had scooters for about one hundred years, but in 1996, the J. D. Corporation in Taiwan made the first lightweight, metal folding scooter — the Razor.

RUBBER TIRES

Many inventions that help people travel from place to place have wheels. The wheel has been around since **prehistoric** times, but the rubber tires used on many wheels are a much more recent invention.

In 1887, John Boyd Dunlop of Scotland trapped air inside a rubber tire to use on his son's tricycle.

Then, in 1895, the Michelin brothers of France made the first air-filled rubber tires for a car.

Since the Michelin brothers' tires, tire manufacturers have developed different types of tires for different vehicles, including snow tires and tires for trucks, tractors, and airplanes.

Time Line

530 B.C.
A picture on a Greek vase shows wheels on a bed.

1490s
Leonardo da Vinci sketches an idea for a helicopter.

1700s
An unknown Dutchman attaches wooden spools to boards under his shoes for the first roller skates.

1769
Scottish engineer James Watt develops the first working steam engine.

Frenchman Nicolas-Joseph Cugnot makes a steam car called the Fardier.

1817
German Baron Karl von Drais Sauerbronn develops the hobbyhorse.

1820s
Horses pull buses in France.

1830
The Baltimore and Ohio Railroad is the first U.S. railroad system.

1863
James Plimpton designs the quad roller skate and opens a roller skating rink in New York City.

1867
Sylvester Howard Roper designs the first steam motorcycle.

1885
John Kemp Starley designs the Rover Safety Bicycle.

Gottlieb Daimler attaches a gas engine to a bicycle frame.

1886
In Germany, Gottlieb Daimler and Wilhelm Mayback build the first gas-powered car.

1888
John Dunlop creates air-filled tires.

1903
The Wright brothers fly the first airplane, in North Carolina.

1907
Frenchman Paul Cornu builds the first working helicopter.

1908
Henry Ford mass-produces the first Model T Fords, in Michigan.

1909
Louis Blériot makes the first flight across the English Channel.

1914
Greyhound buses begin taking passengers from city to city.

1918
The Autoped Company of America makes the first motor scooter.

George Westinghouse patents an electric wheelchair in New York.

1927
U.S. aviator Charles Lindbergh flies across the Atlantic Ocean.

1936
The Cushman Company makes motor scooters for the U.S. Army.

1939
Germany's He178 is the first jet engine to fly.

1948
England hosts the first wheelchair games as a sporting event.

1960s
Plastic wheels make roller skates lighter and easier to use.

1964
Japan builds the Bullet train.

1969
Boeing builds the 747 "Jumbo Jet."

1970s
Outdoor enthusiasts modify their bicycles to make mountain bikes.

1976
France's Concorde supersonic airplane carries passengers for the first time.

1980
Scott and Brennan Olson make new in-line skates called Rollerblades®.

1986
Westland Lynx breaks the world helicopter speed record by flying 250 miles (402 km) per hour.

1997
Toyota sells the Prius, the first gas-electric hybrid car, in Japan.

2003
The Independence® iBOT® wheelchair can climb stairs.

Glossary

all-terrain
able to run on-road and off-road. An all-terrain vehicle can travel on unpaved surfaces.

assembly line
a way that people make things, using a line of people and machines that put items together in a certain order so that each person or machine has just one job

aviator
a person who flies an airplane; a pilot

axle
the pin or rod that runs through the center of a wheel. The wheel turns around the axle.

coal
a natural black solid that is burned as fuel

competitions
contests or games played to win

develop
to make something better

device
a piece of equipment designed to do a certain task

engineer
a scientist who studies, designs, and builds machines, buildings, or other products

enthusiasts
people who are very interested in, and enjoy, a certain activity

gears
the parts of a bicycle that determine the speed at which the wheels turn around

historians
people who study and write about history

hybrid
describes a car or a motorcycle that uses more than one type of power, such as a combination of gas and electricity

in-line
having wheels set in a straight line

inexpensive
does not cost a lot of money

invalid
a person who has a long-term illness or disability

paraplegic
a person who cannot move the lower part of his or her body and usually needs to use a wheelchair

patents
claims the ownership rights to an invention so that it cannot be copied

prehistoric
the time long before written history

quad
four

rotary
capable of turning like a wheel

steady wheels
smaller wheels that are attached to the sides of the back wheel of a bicycle or motorcycle to help keep the bike upright and steady

steering column
the pole found on a bicycle, car, motorcycle, or scooter that attaches to a wheel or handle bars for steering

solo
alone

supersonic
faster than the speed of sound

Further Information

Books

Transportation Then and Now. First Step Nonfiction (series). Robin Nelson (Lerner)

Travel in the Early Days. Historic Communities (series). Bobbie Kalman and Kate Calder (Crabtree)

Web Sites

Famous people: George Stephenson. www.bbc.co.uk/schools/famouspeople/standard/stephenson/

America on the Move: Games www.americanhistory.si.edu/onthemove/games/

Publisher's note to educators and parents: Our editors have carefully reviewed these Web sites to ensure that they are suitable for children. Many Web sites change frequently, however, and we cannot guarantee that a site's future contents will continue to meet our high standards of quality and educational value. Be advised that children should be closely supervised whenever they access the Internet.

31

Index